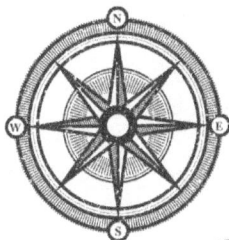

Burning Ships

LEAD THE LIFE YOU
WERE MADE TO LIVE

DOUGLAS C. MANN

HOUSEGRAVITY

BURNING SHIPS
ISBN 978-0-578-40184-3
Copyright © 2018 by Douglas C. Mann
Cover Design by Design9Studios
Compass Illustration by Vecteezy.com

Published in the United States of America by House Gravity

Cataloging-in-Publication data for this book is available from the Library of Congress

Printed in the United States of America
2018 – First Edition

For our Zoya McKenna

Presented to

_____

from

_____

on

_____

Not All Who Wander Are Lost

CONTENTS

HOW TO USE THIS GUIDED JOURNAL

Wondering how to get started on your journey into new discoveries, a new world, and new you? That's exactly why I created this guided journal. My hope is it will act as a guiding marker to help you reframe your approach to life, chart a new course and truly help you lead the life you were made to live.

Each section begins with a short narrative, followed by space to reflect, an area to consider how best to chart your course as you progress and room to write any *a-ha!* moments, which I refer to as new discoveries. You'll come across practical and interactive prompts to enhance your experience, and blank journal pages for you to fill in.

Remember, every journey begins with a single step of faith. Determine to not only chase your dreams, but catch them, and live them out. Journey on and journey well.

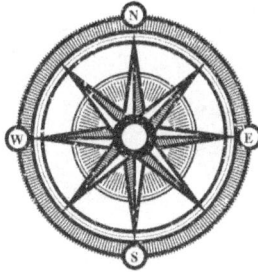

Your Destiny is Not Determined by Chance.
It is Determined by Choice.

INTRODUCTION

Daring explorers have always set out for the "New Worlds" – the Norse explorer Leif Erikson, the female Icelandic explorer, Gudridur, who helped colonize North America, Amelia Earhart, the famous aviator who traversed the globe and Ferninand Magellan, who became the first to navigate the earth, launching the age of discovery.

Almost one-thousand years earlier, Alexander the Great landed on Persian shores and burned his ships, committing his forces to victory or defeat. Spanish conquistador explorer, Hernan Cortez scuttled his fleet of ships off the Veracruz coast, stranding his expedition in the Americas. It's said that Cortez delivered an impassioned speech to his expedition and ended with the spirited command, "Burn the boats!"

Maybe like the early explorers, we need to navigate into uncharted territories to find our "New Worlds," to journey and launch our personal age of discovery. That is, to burn our ships like those who came before us, to do away with any thought of turning back and progressing forward as our only option. While it may not be a very comforting thought, perserverance and resolve like this is necessary to prevent wavering in our determination, self-discovery, and self-development.

Sure, everyone wants to be great like Alexander or Cortez, but none of us want to burn our ships. We prefer to sip our drinks poolside and reminisce about the good old days.

But we all have ships to burn. Their christened names are Fear, Pride, Arrogance, Acclaim, Lost Love, maybe even Approval Seeker or People Pleaser.

Are your christened ships anchored offshore in a secure pristine harbor? Do you want to lead the life you were made to live? If so, give the resolute yet heartening command, "Burn the boats!" It's time to join the adventure and explore uncharted life territories. We cannot change our past, but we can change our future.

Years ago, I launched my own personal age of discovery. Part renaissance man and global wanderer, the words of J. R. R. Tolkien, "Not all those who wander are lost," encouraged and assured me throughout the peaks and valleys of my journey. May it be the same for you.

Read on, journal on, and journey into new discoveries and the uncharted territory of a new world, and new you.

Doug

Douglas Christopher Mann

RISK OR RUST

There is a well-founded adage, "risk or rust." That is, risk nothing, say nothing, do nothing.

Our lives are defined by decisive moments, which have a ripple effect through time. When we fail to act, we alter if not relinquish the future.

Like any uncharted passage, there may be some risks and adversity along the way. But with adversity comes opportunity.

Early explorers navigated by the stars and sea, the Norse by sunstone to polarize light in order to assess and determine their direction. Seafaring mariners were guided by a magnetized needle, which aligned itself with the magnetic fields of the earth.

Despite all the unknowns, all the challenging encounters, none turned back. Nor should you. Resist any thoughts to waver, be resolute, forge ahead and lean into your future.

REFLECTIONS

Describe the life you desire. Then list what it is holding you
back.

_____

_____

_____

_____

_____

_____

_____

_____

_____

_____

_____

_____

_____

_____

_____

_____

_____

_____

"What you choose to do will shape who you are."

CHART YOUR LIFE COURSE

Now that you've identified the things holding you back,
what can you do to remove these obstacles from your path?

_____

_____

_____

_____

_____

_____

_____

_____

_____

_____

_____

_____

_____

_____

_____

Brainstorm goals you are determined to pursue.

NEW DISCOVERIES

What's one thing you've learned. Include any *ah-ha!* moments and write them here.

_____

_____

_____

_____

_____

_____

_____

_____

_____

_____

_____

_____

_____

_____

_____

_____

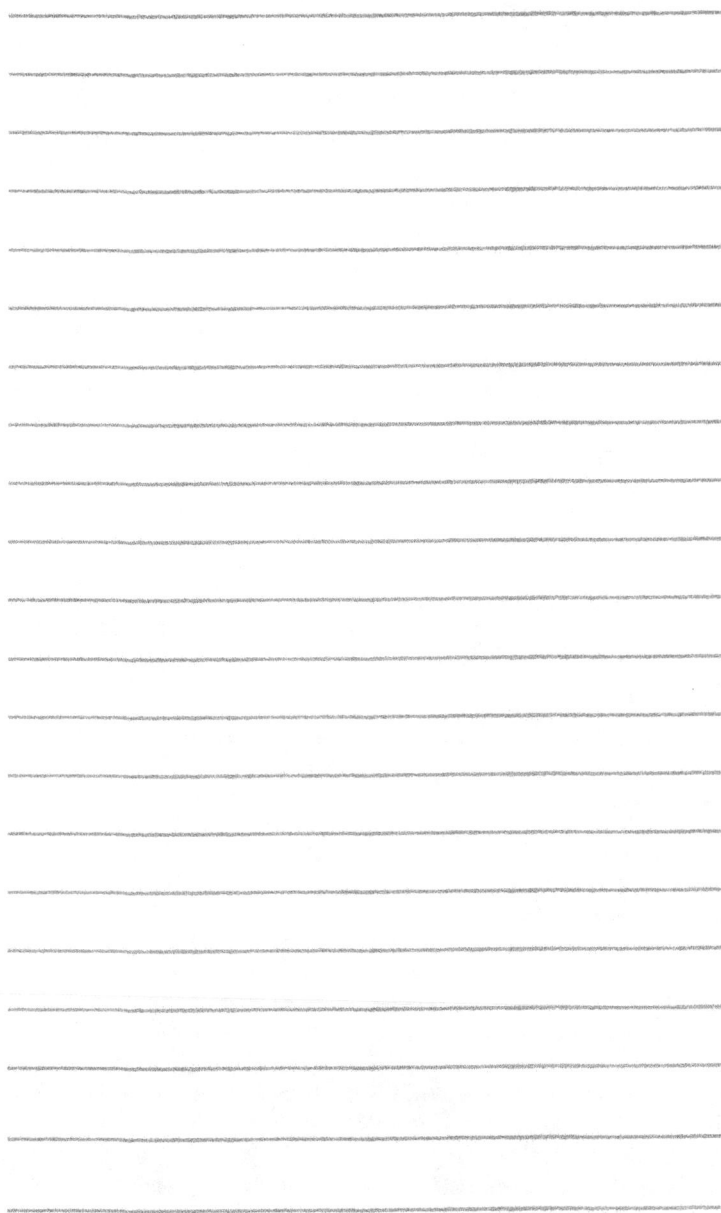

JOURNALING

Think of what you're doing as a way to reframe your approach to life. Write down your thoughts and feelings. Reflect on each one to better understand them more clearly. Acknowledge and embrace those that encourage you.

"To begin, begin." – William Wordsworth

KNOW YOUR TRUE NORTH

By definition, True North is an imaginary line, which runs parallel to the earth's axis. In locating this, one can find a fixed marker, proceed in the right direction and properly navigate toward a destination.

Finding your True North is essential for accurate life navigation. This enables you to align who you are and what you believe. It is owning and living by your own definition and terms, not someone else's. It's understanding what your truth is and ultimately, the path you are to follow.

Your True North is a fixed point. It is an internal compass to help orient you, to steadily navigate and stay on course in what can often be a tumultuous world.

This may mean purposefully practicing mindfulness. Take time to slow down and be attentive to your life, all that surrounds you. Practice listening not only with your ears, but also with your heart.

In essence, True North increases your clarity and ability to live a more meaningful life.

REFLECTIONS

What core values and life perspectives matter most to you? Which need to be your fixed points to plot your course and determine your True North?

_____

_____

_____

_____

_____

_____

_____

_____

_____

_____

_____

_____

_____

_____

"Freedom is the courage to be yourself."

CHART YOUR LIFE COURSE

What in your life may compromise or alter your desired course?

_____

_____

_____

_____

_____

_____

_____

_____

_____

_____

_____

_____

_____

_____

_____

When you're in need of a significant course correction, how will you deal with that tension to reorient yourself?

NEW DISCOVERIES

What's one thing you've learned. Include any *ah-ha!* moments and write them here.

_____

_____

_____

_____

_____

_____

_____

_____

_____

_____

_____

_____

_____

_____

_____

_____

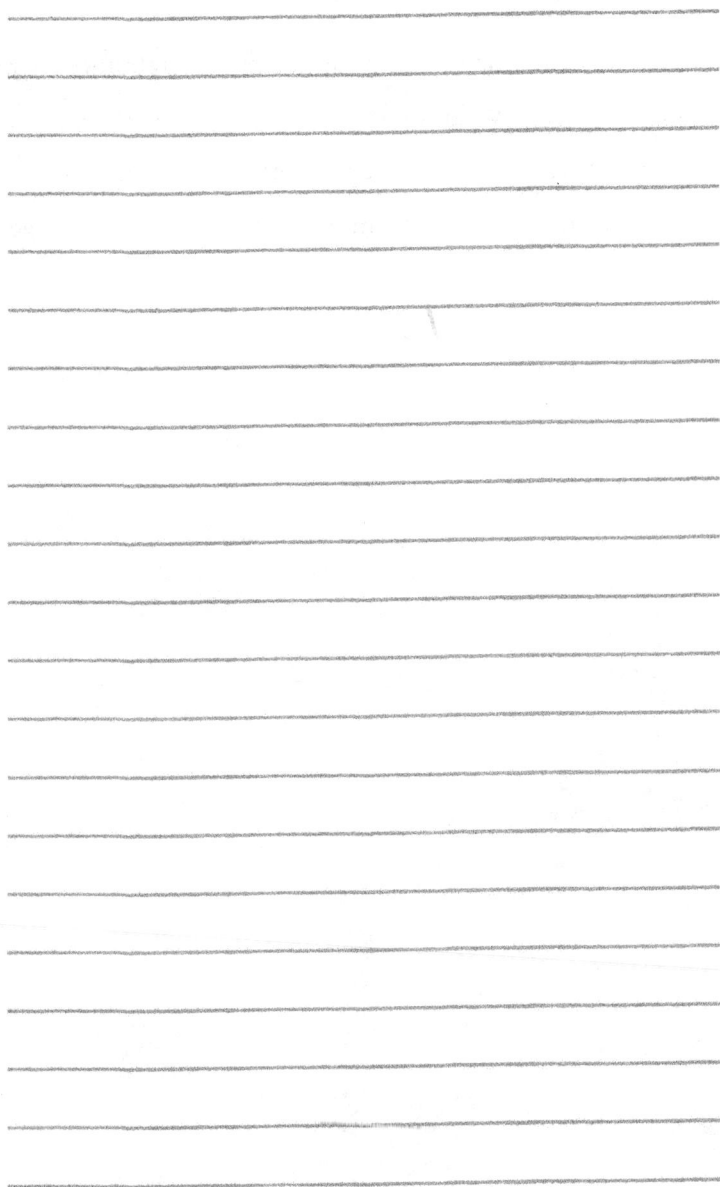

JOURNALING

Think of what you're doing as a way to reframe your approach to life. Write down your thoughts and feelings. Reflect on each one to better understand them more clearly. Acknowledge and embrace those that encourage you.

_____

_____

_____

_____

_____

_____

_____

_____

_____

_____

_____

_____

_____

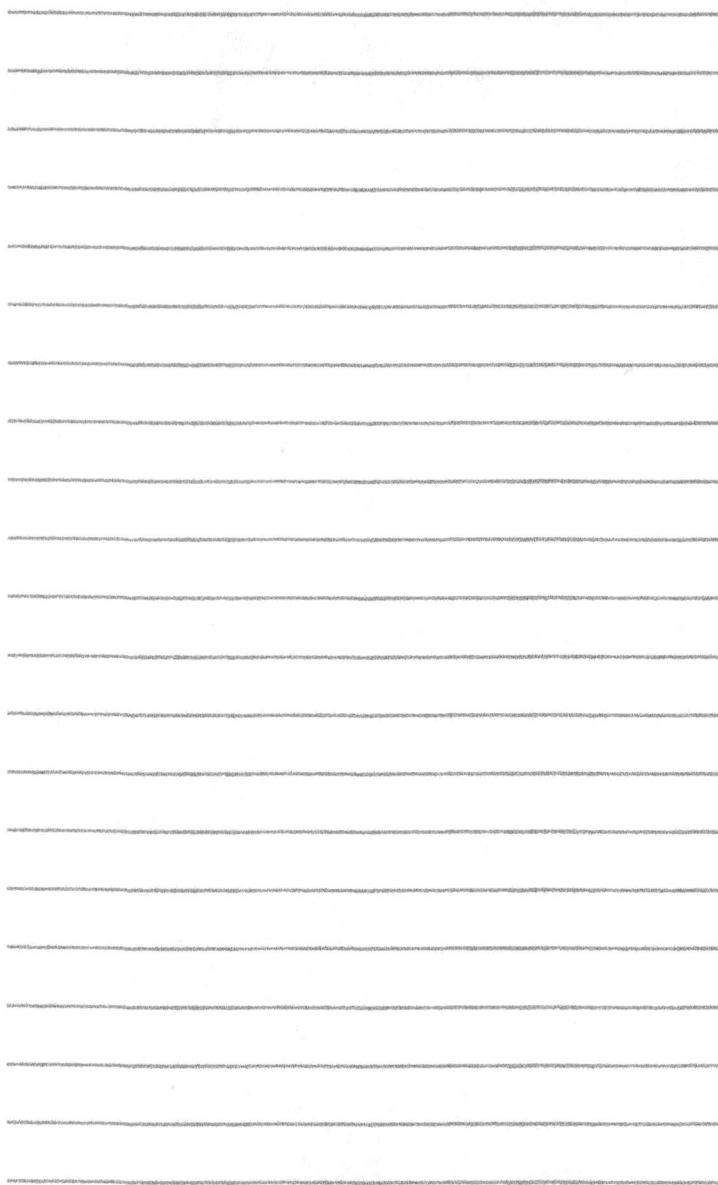

*"You may not find yourself where intended,
but you are where you need to be."*

DESTINY IS DETERMINED BY CHOICE. NOT CHANCE.

Are you not only willing, but ready to trade *what if* for *why not?* There's something about the definitive invitation of why not beckoning in the distance, across the horizon, "What are you waiting for?"

Answering that call is to set the process of your future in motion. This is a pivotal moment in your life. It is where you discover and come to understand that this new found freedom is actually the courage to truly be yourself.

Your hopes, your dreams, your future awaits your single-mindedness; your decisive course of action.

Your destiny is not a mystery; it is a moment of decision in the present. It is determined by choice, not by chance. Seize it this very day!

REFLECTIONS

List the *what if's* that dominate your life.

_____

_____

_____

_____

_____

_____

_____

_____

_____

_____

_____

_____

_____

_____

_____

Now, write which of these should become *why not's.*

_____

_____

_____

_____

_____

_____

_____

_____

_____

_____

_____

_____

_____

*"Be inspired. Be consistent.
Be what you are intended to be."*

CHART YOUR LIFE COURSE

What actionable steps will you take to make your *why not's* reality?

_____

_____

_____

_____

_____

_____

_____

_____

_____

_____

_____

_____

_____

_____

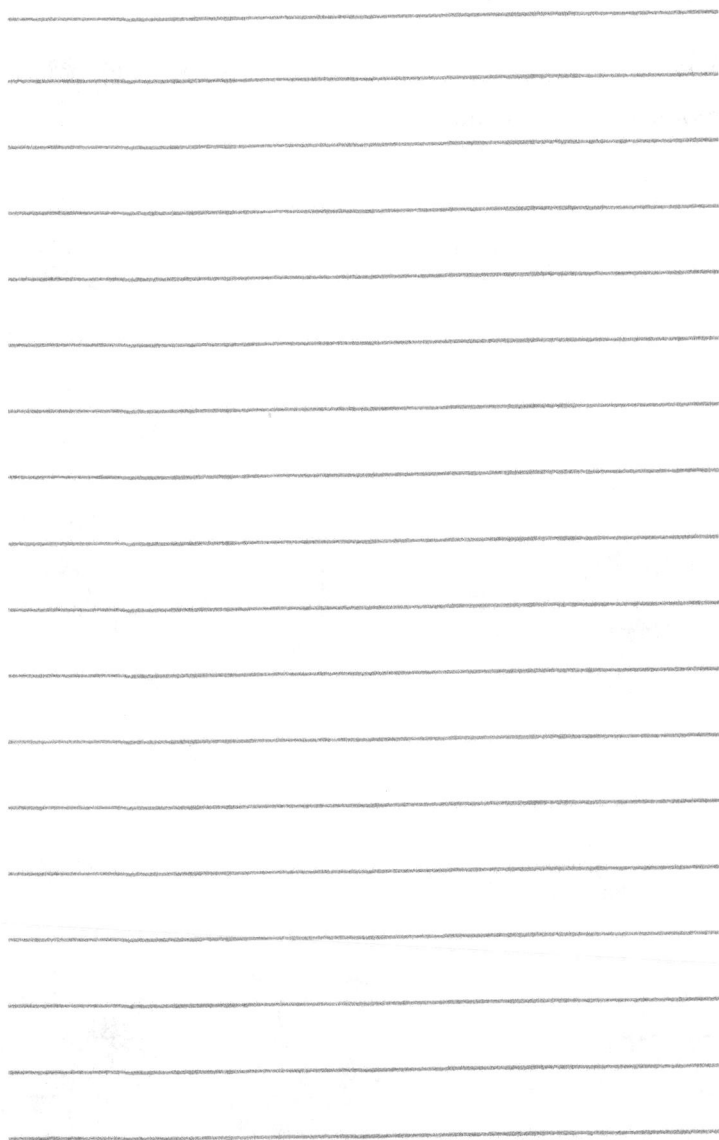

NEW DISCOVERIES

What's one thing you've learned. Include any *ah-ha!* moments and write them here.

_____

_____

_____

_____

_____

_____

_____

_____

_____

_____

_____

_____

_____

_____

_____

_____

_____

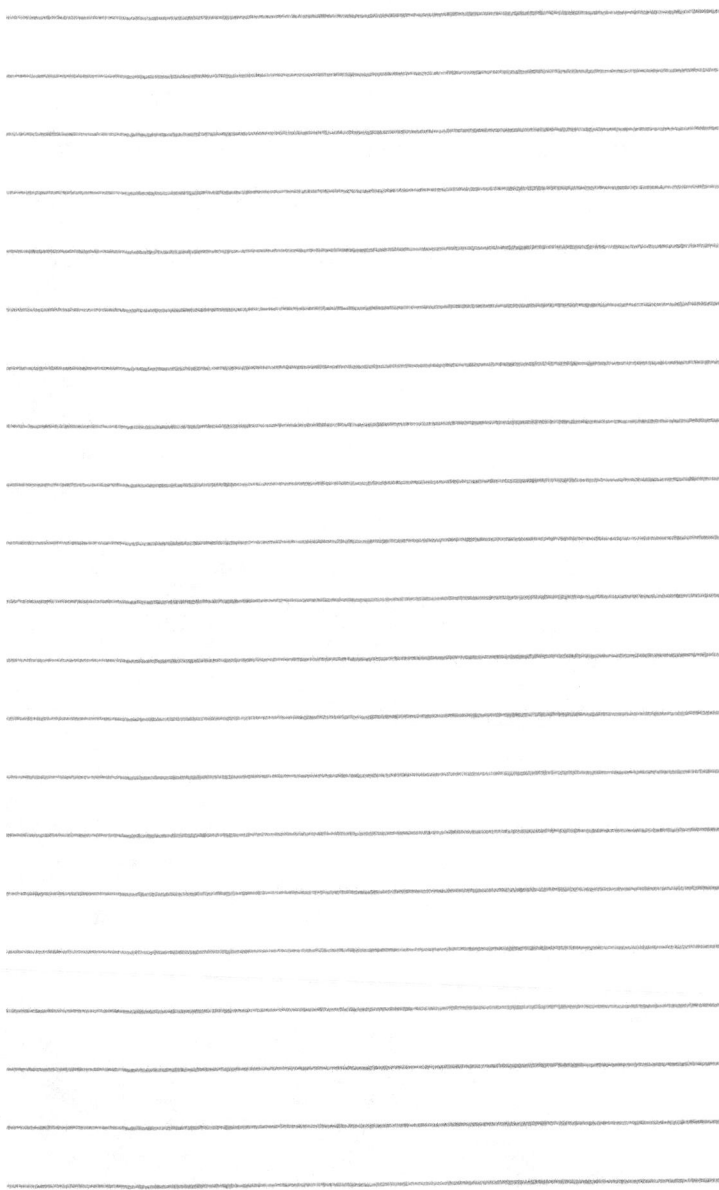

JOURNALING

Think of what you're doing as a way to reframe your approach to life. Write down your thoughts and feelings. Reflect on each one to better understand them more clearly. Acknowledge and embrace those that encourage you.

_____

_____

_____

_____

_____

_____

_____

_____

_____

_____

_____

_____

_____

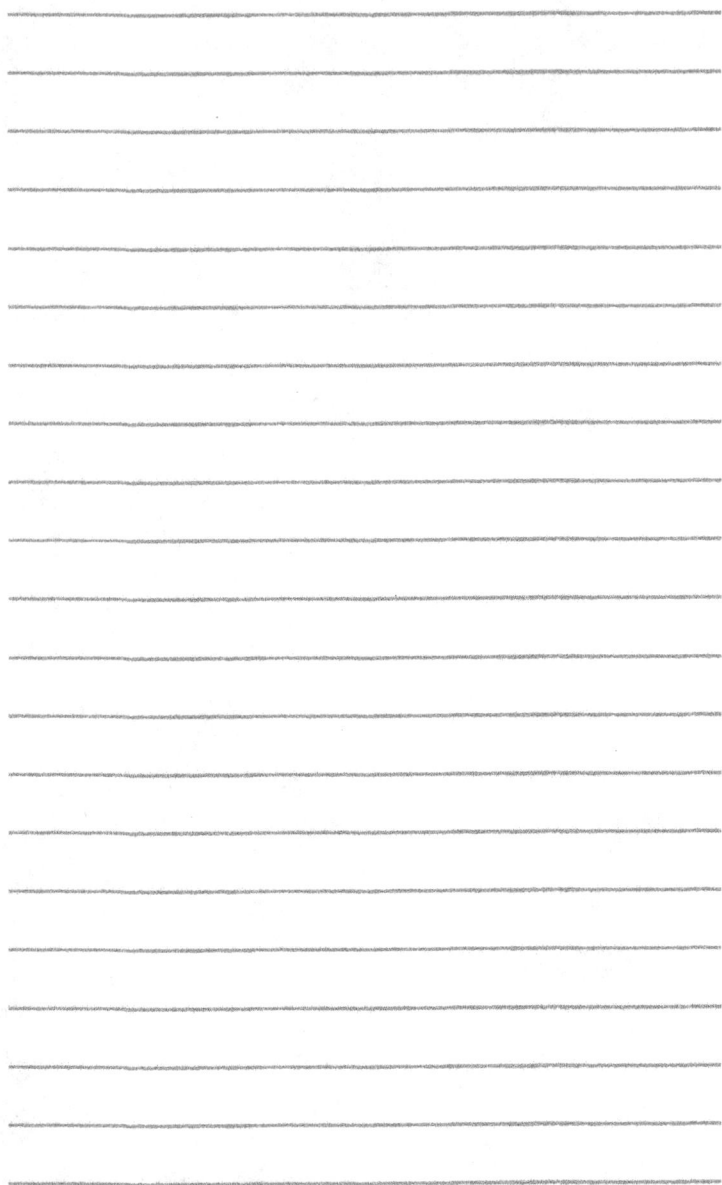

"Every journey begins with a single step of faith."

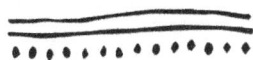

TRAVEL A CONSTANT PATH OF DISCOVERY AND CHANGE

This is *your* time, *your* age of discovery. Be inquisitive and courageous; explore, and break new ground in unknown realms in search of your "New World."

Approach this time with a sense of wonder and look to expand your world-view. Dimiss any preconceived notions or opinions. Expect mountaintop moments and also valleys with hidden obstacles; it is part of the transformation process.

Leo Tolstoy said, "Everyone thinks of changing the world but no one thinks of changing himself." In the spirit of this, first change yourself – then change the world.

Chronicle your life-changing pilgrimage on these pages. Describe what it looks and feels like, even some of the unexpected and surprising diversions you have encountered or are experiencing.

Perhaps there are lessons to be learned from each of these, ones you may want to take particular note of.

REFLECTIONS

What are some of the things you have encountered or are experiencing? Describe what you hope it is to discover.

_____

_____

_____

_____

_____

_____

_____

_____

_____

_____

_____

_____

_____

"Define commitment as a verb, not merely a noun."

CHART YOUR LIFE COURSE

List the things you do that matter most *to you*. Which give your life more meaning?

NEW DISCOVERIES

What's one thing you've learned. Include any *ah-ha!* moments and write them here.

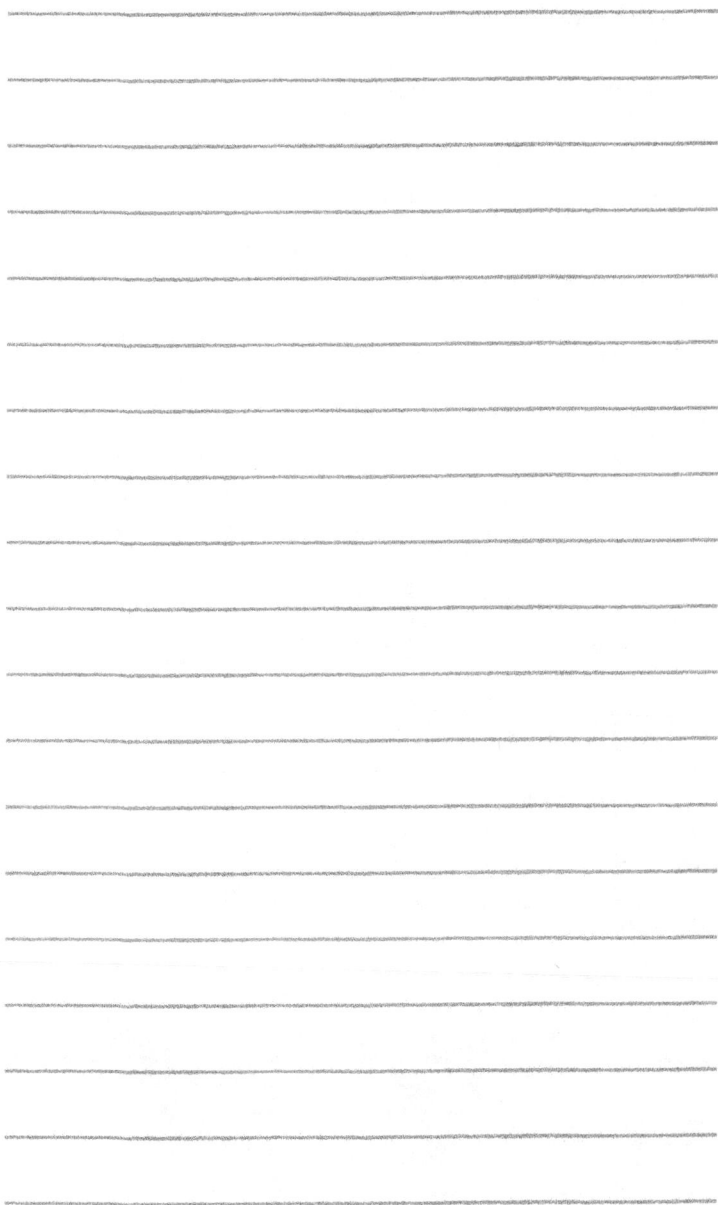

JOURNALING

Think of what you're doing as a way to reframe your approach to life. Write down your thoughts and feelings. Reflect on each one to better understand them more clearly. Acknowledge and embrace those that encourage you.

_____

_____

_____

_____

_____

_____

_____

_____

_____

_____

_____

_____

*"It doesn't matter how long your journey is.
Always continue and never stop."*

ASSESS YOUR JOURNEY

Like all explorers, you should periodically check the progress of your chosen course. You want to be certain you are heading in the right direction.

Write what your life-location looks like? Include any adjustments to your goals to ensure you stay on course.

_____

_____

_____

_____

_____

_____

_____

_____

_____

_____

_____

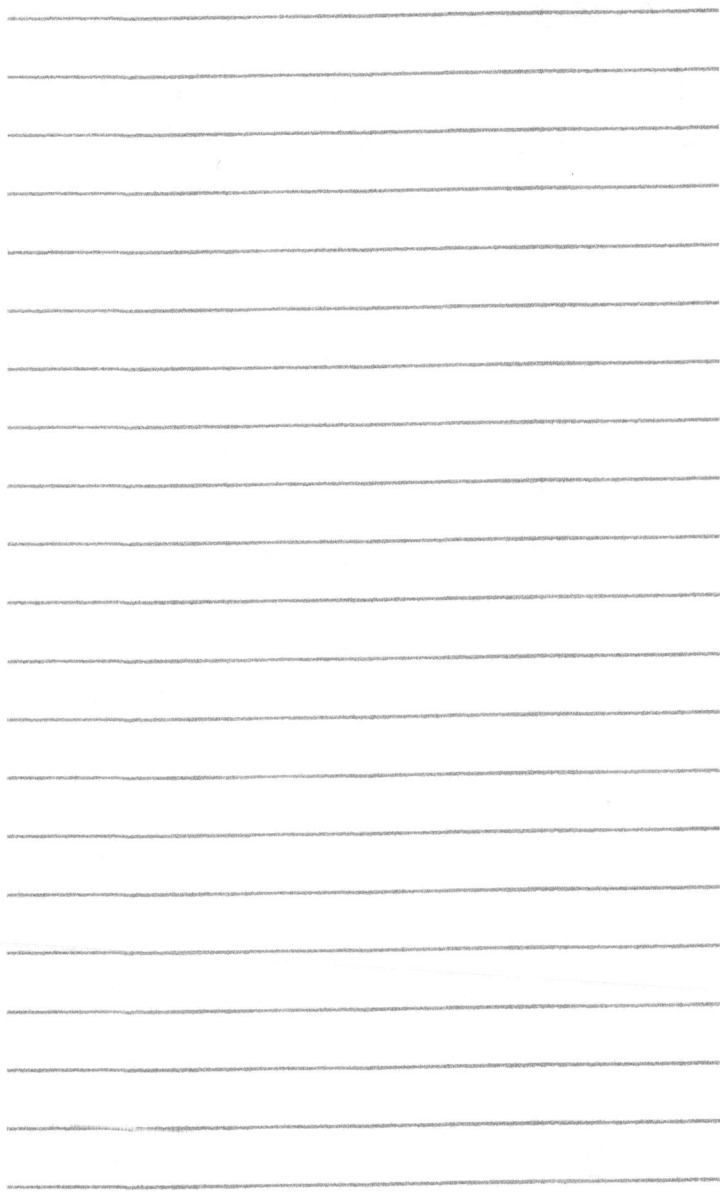

SUCCESS STORIES

List any accomplishments you feel you have achieved. Check each circle as a way to acknowledge them.

○

_____

_____

_____

_____

_____

○

_____

_____

_____

_____

_____

_____

"Celebrate well. Journey on."

LEARN FROM YOUR PAST.
DON'T LIVE IN IT.

People don't always like change so most are more than glad to remind you of your past. Whether realized or not, they are operating from their own fear-based insecurities. But you don't have to accept or own it. Many will tell you what you cannot do. Don't be one of them.

You have the power to change your future. What you choose to do will shape who you are. This means caring enough for your present self to move beyond regrets and leave your past behind.

Often, it's difficult to know which bridges to cross and which to burn. One of the most challenging bridges to burn is the one to your past self. But some bridges are worth burning.

And just like bridges, we all have ships to burn. Their christened names may be Fear, Pride, Arrogance, Approval Seeker or People Pleaser.

Know you are enough and abandon what you have accepted as the status quo of your past. Indecision is your adversary. Choose to no longer allow it to be your decision.

Determine to not only chase your dreams, but catch them, and live them out. You are your own dreamcatcher.

REFLECTIONS

List the christened names of your ships to burn.

_____

_____

_____

_____

_____

_____

_____

_____

_____

_____

"Many people will tell you what you cannot do.
Don't be one of them."

CHART YOUR LIFE COURSE

Write the names of your christened ships on separate pieces of paper. Now is the time to dispatch them with a sense of immediacy.

You may want to safely burn them or purposefully tear each into tiny pieces, toss the scraps over your shoulder and walk away. Or maybe you prefer to power-shred each with a sense of intentionality.

What matters most is the act of discarding these named things that have weighed you down and held you back for far too long. Do this and create a positive release of energy and forward momentum for yourself.

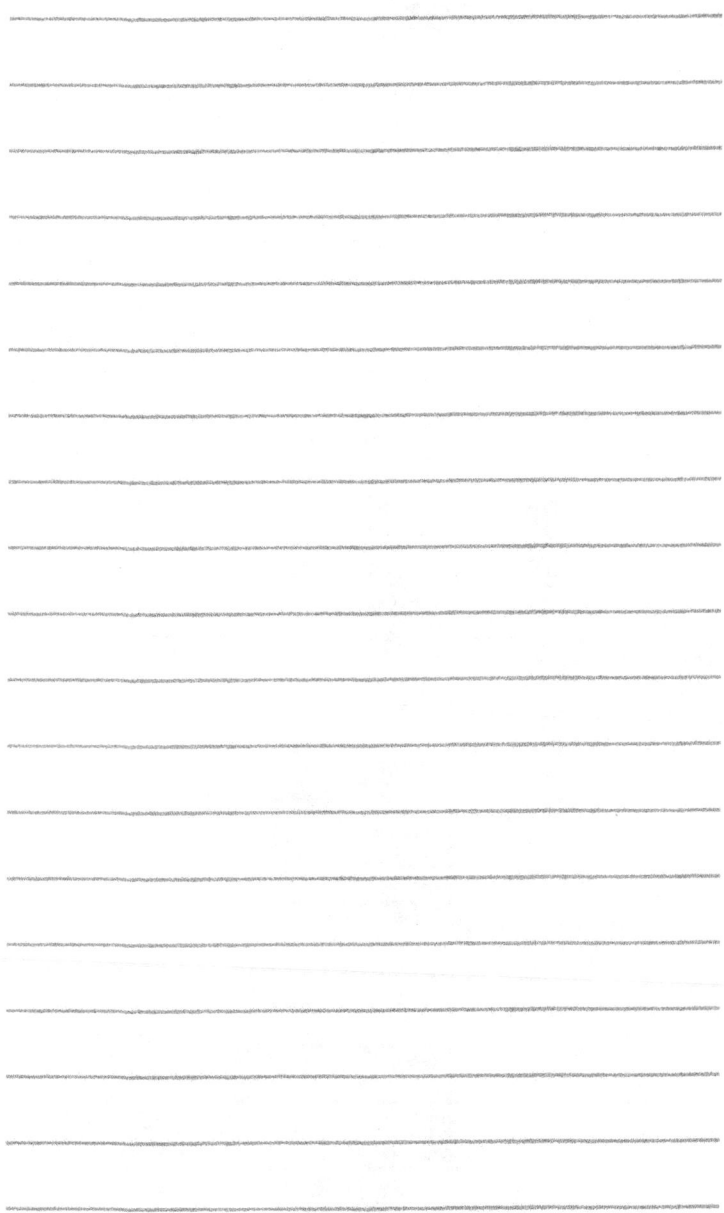

NEW DISCOVERIES

What's one thing you've learned. Include any *ah-ha!* moments and write them here.

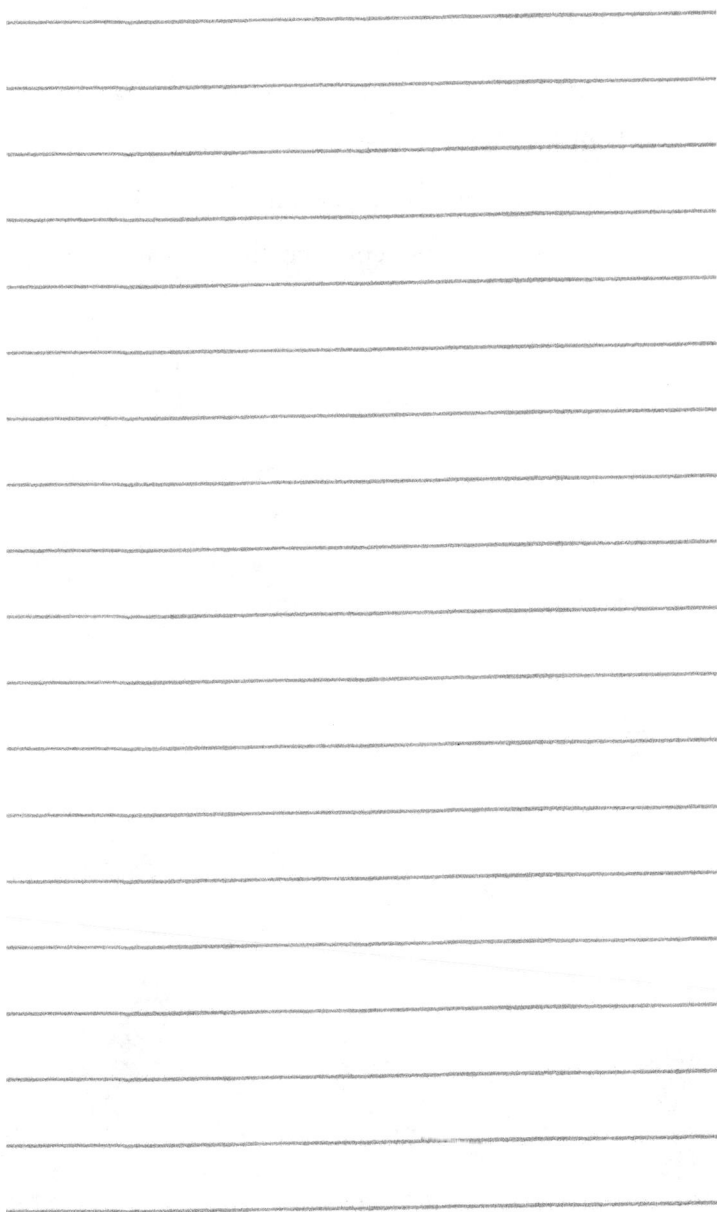

JOURNALING

Think of what you're doing as a way to reframe your approach to life. Write down your thoughts and feelings. Reflect on each one to better understand them more clearly. Acknowledge and embrace those that encourage you.

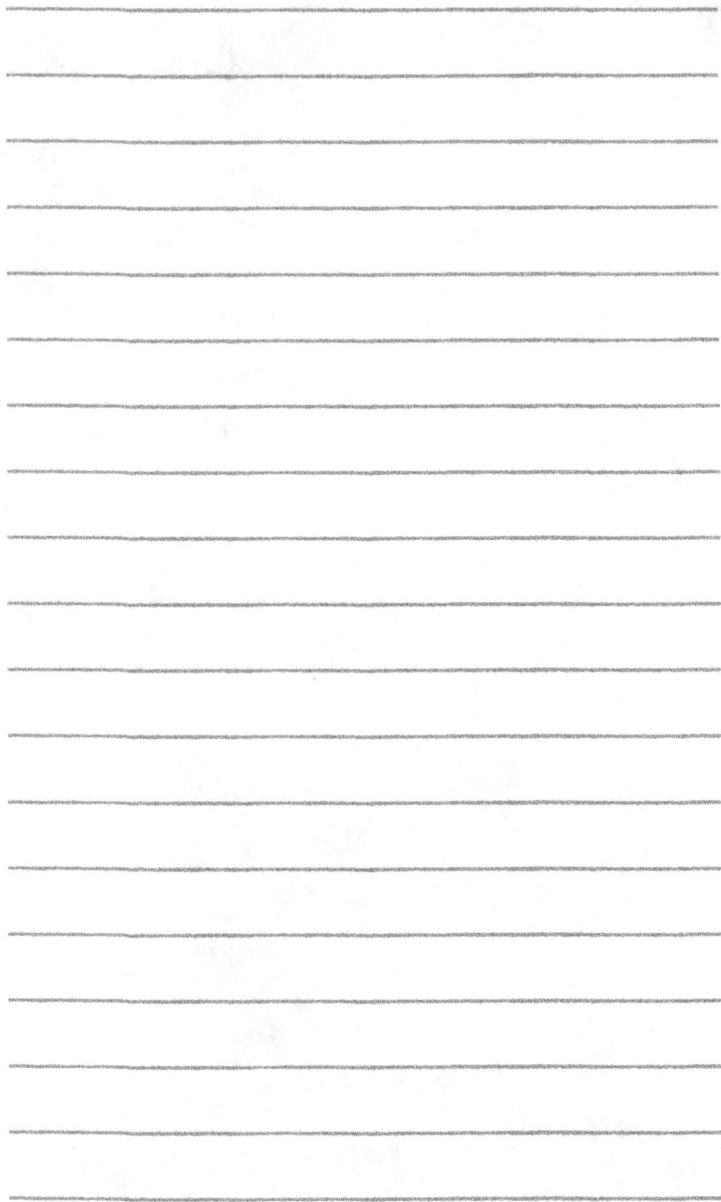

"Some bridges really are worth burning."

LEAD THE LIFE YOU WERE MADE TO LIVE

Reflect on your own expedition of discovery. Think of all the personal progress you have made and acknowledge identifiable areas of transformation in your life. As you press on, all that is required is the daily decision to purposefully move forward, explore, learn and live.

Be mindful, it is an ongoing choice to be compassionate and kind to yourself. Be grateful, for it puts life into true perspective.

Continue to choose to make real life changes, to improve your life and those around you. Leave a lasting legacy. That is what faith in action looks like.

Persevere in what you have started. Let the doubters doubt, for that is all they know to do. Always remember – believe in yourself, be a positive force and lead the life you were made to live.

REFLECTIONS

Take time to reflect on the defining moments in your journey. What three things stand out the most?

_____

_____

_____

_____

_____

_____

_____

_____

_____

_____

_____

_____

_____

_____

"Don't only write the stories of your life, but live them out."

CHART YOUR LIFE COURSE

What most do you want to be known for now?

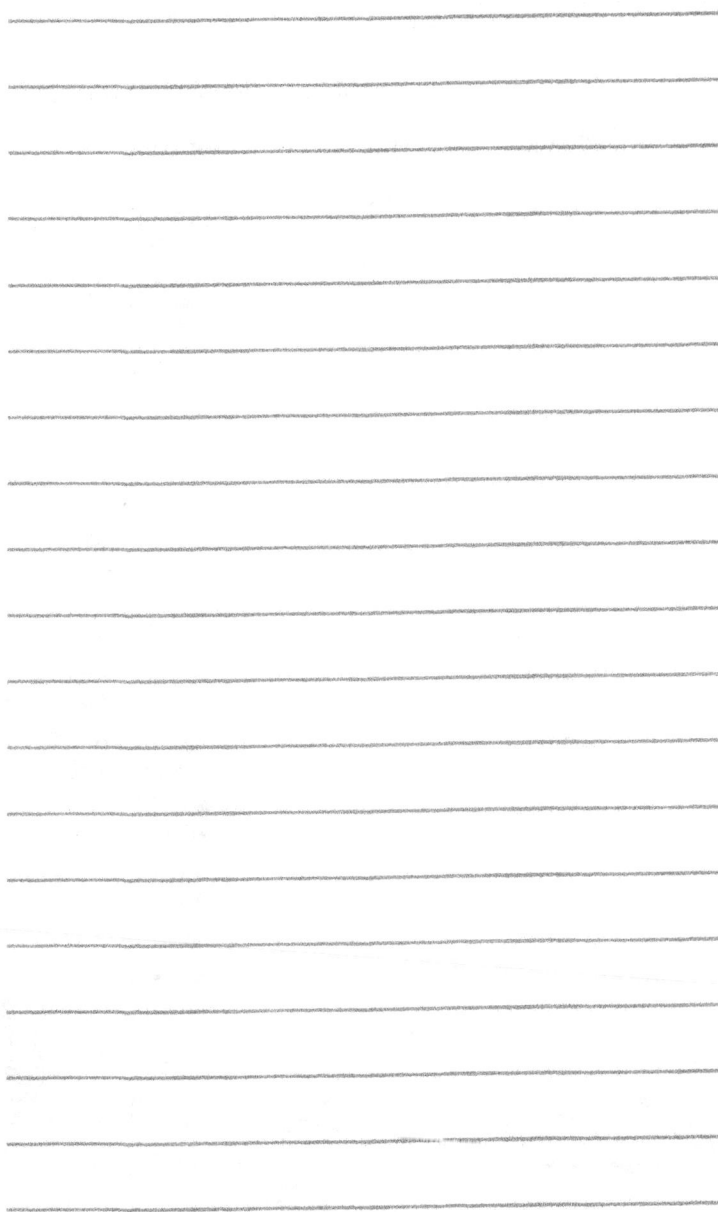

NEW DISCOVERIES

Write the most poignant *ah-ha!* moments you have experienced during your expedition of discovery.

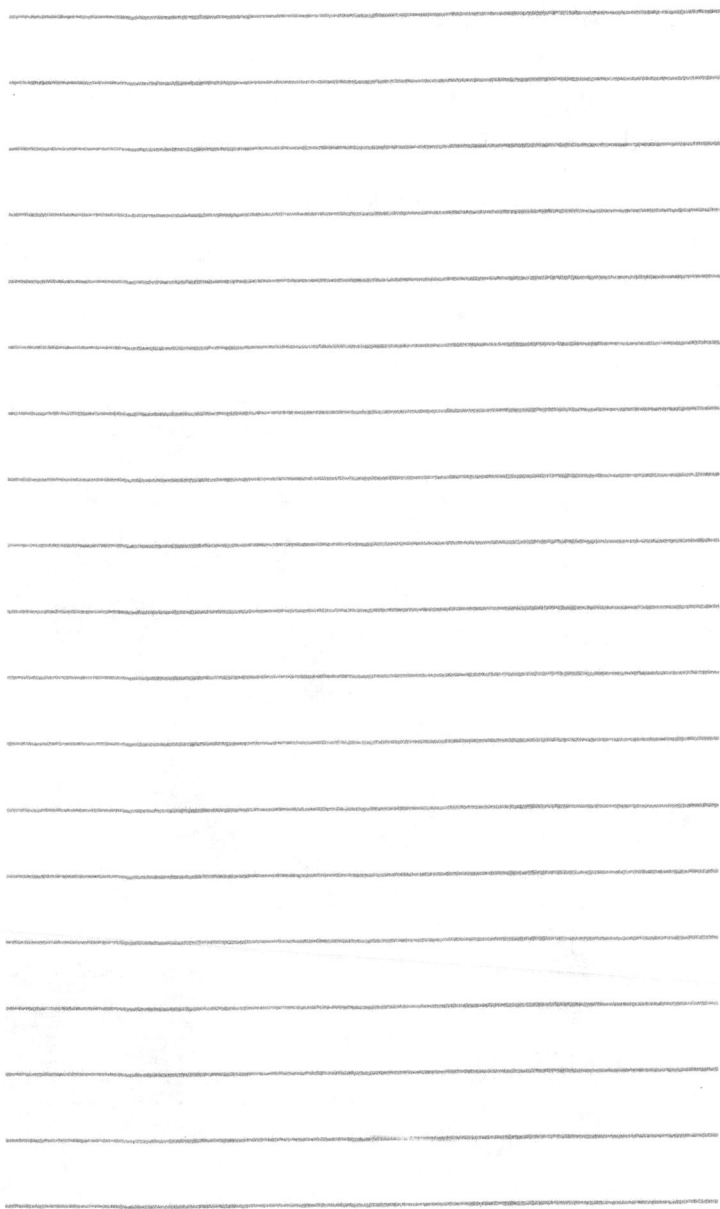

JOURNALING

Write the most prominent ways you have reframed your approach to life. When you're done, read each aloud. Acknowledge them and check each circle.

◯

_____

_____

_____

_____

_____

_____

◯

_____

_____

_____

_____

_____

"Journey on. Journey well."

WRITE YOUR STORY

Look back from where you have come. Recognize the significant progress you have made. Integrate and weave your experiences into a meaningful life narrative, and capture them on these pages. Include all the twists and turns, the things you have discovered about yourself, and also your optimism for the future.

Drop a reminder into your calendar to periodically prompt you to revisit your journal entries in this guide.

_____

_____

_____

_____

_____

_____

_____

_____

_____

_____

"The power of your story is writing it."

"The power of your story is writing it."

"The power of your story is writing it."

"The power of your story is writing it."

LIVE YOUR STORY

While writing about your story is good and needed, living it out is even better! You have shown you are not interested in settling for an ordinary life. You have determined to live an extraordinary life, one filled with purposeful passion and commitment.

There is no better time than now to begin living in the moment and being spontaneous. What are some of the ways you will now live your story?

_____

_____

_____

_____

_____

_____

_____

_____

_____

_____

"The power of your story is living it."

"The power of your story is living it."

"The power of your story is living it."

"The power of your story is living it."

SHARE YOUR STORY

Is there someone who comes to mind that may benefit by hearing your story? Telling others about it could be the nudge of inspiration and encouragement needed for them to launch their own expedition of discovery.

Write on these pages what it is you would say to them.

"The power of your story is sharing it."

"The power of your story is sharing it."

"The power of your story is sharing it."

"The power of your story is sharing it."

Journey on. Journey well.

RECOMMENDED READS

Books that inspired me on my personal journey

The Annotated Walden
ASIN: B009F1L4HS
Library of Congress Catalog Card Number: 76-118296
Henry David Thoreau
Bramhall House, a division of Clarkson N. Potter, Inc., 1970

The Poetic Edda
ISBN: 9781624663567
Jackson Crawford
Hackett Publishing Company, 2015

Reckoning with Dust
ISBN: 9780999469002
Jennifer Pirecki
Redfern Ink, 2017

We Stood Upon Stars
ISBN: 9781601429599
Roger W. Thompson
WaterBrook, 2017

9780578401843